Boscobel House and White Ladies Priory

SHROPSHIRE

O J WEAVER MA, FSA,

with essays by R Gilyard-Beer OBE, MA, FSA and J J West BPhil, MA

Boscobel House is a modest timber framed building in a quiet part of Shropshire; a building, one would think, little disturbed by the tumult of national events. But for one brief period of its history it gave shelter to King Charles II after the rout of his army at Worcester in September 1651, and so played a crucial role in an event that has since become a famous part of our history. There are few, perhaps, who have not heard of the oak tree nearby in whose branches Charles sheltered to escape capture, or of his perilous journey to Bristol afterwards disguised as a servant.

This guidebook tells the story of those events. It also contains a description of Boscobel House, a note on the oak tree, and a history of Boscobel in the nineteenth century, when it came to be valued for its romantic associations. The nearby house at White Ladies, where Charles took refuge initially after his defeat, has long since disappeared, but on the site are the ruins of a nunnery which once formed part of the house, and they are also described in this book.

Contents

Unless otherwise stated illustrations are copyright English Heritage and the photographs were taken by the English Heritage Photographic Unit (Photo Library: 01793 414903)

Published by English Heritage
Waterhouse Square, 138-142 Holborn, London EC1N 2ST
© English Heritage 1987
First published 1987, reprinted 1988, 1993
Second edition 1996, reprinted 2001, 2005, 2007, 2009
Printed in England by Pureprint Group
C30 03/09 05554
ISBN 978-1-85074-623-2

Visit our website at www.english-heritage.org.uk

Mixed Sources
Product group from well-managed forests, controlled sources and recycled wood or fiber
www.fsc.org Cert no. SGS-COC-0620
© 1996 Forest Stewardship Council
FSC

Charles II, Boscobel and White Ladies

The farmhouse and the main house from the east (see the plan on page 18)

To set the scene for the events at Boscobel it is necessary to go back in time to 30 January 1649 when, after more than six years of civil war, King Charles I was beheaded in front of his palace of Whitehall. England was declared a Commonwealth, a new government was set up and the country was without a king for eleven years.

Charles I, however, had a son, the young Prince Charles, who had fled from England during the Civil War, taking shelter first in France and later in Holland. It was merely a matter of time before he attempted to regain his father's throne and in the summer of 1650, shortly after his twentieth birthday, he set sail from Holland and landed in Scotland on 23 June. On 1 January 1651 he was crowned at Scone but it was a hollow ceremony, a gesture of defiance rather than a mark of victory. His Scottish forces had already been soundly defeated by Oliver Cromwell, Edinburgh was taken, and all that was left to Charles was the desperate expedient of riding south into England with what remained of his army, hoping that the country would rally to his side.

He reached Worcester on 22 August 1651 virtually unopposed but, of greater significance, having gathered very few new supporters on his way. On 23 August in Worcester he was proclaimed "King of Great Britain, France and Ireland," and on the same day summoned a general

3

Charles's route after the Battle of Worcester

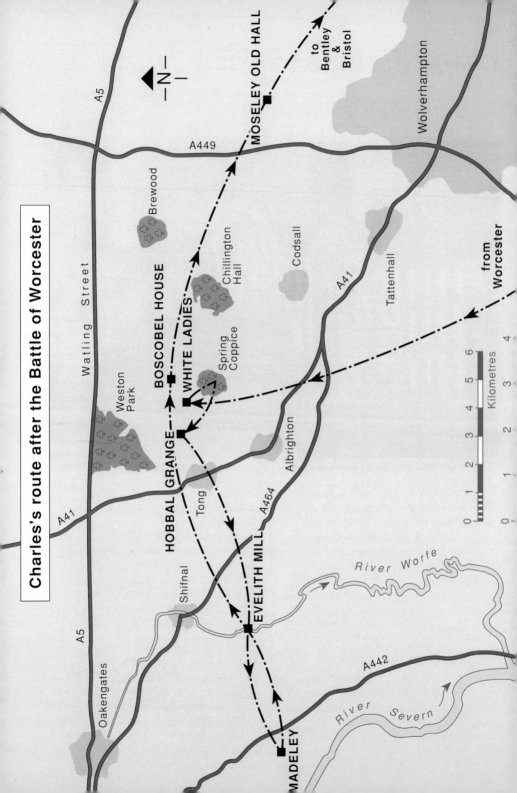

N

A5

Watling Street

A449

Brewood

MOSELEY OLD HALL

to
Bentley
&
Bristol

Wolverhampton

BOSCOBEL HOUSE

WHITE LADIES

Chillington
Hall

Codsall

Spring
Coppice

A41

Tattenhall

from
Worcester

Weston
Park

HOBBAL GRANGE

A5

A41

Tong

Albrighton

Kilometres
0 1 2 3 4 5 6

Shifnal

A464

EVELITH MILL

Oakengates

River Worfe

A442

MADELEY

River Severn

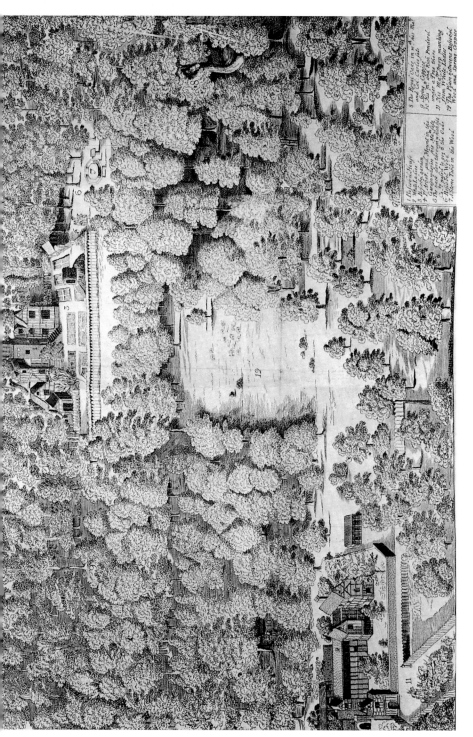

Engraving by Wenceslas Hollar for Thomas Blount's Boscobel (1660). The distance between Boscobel House (top) and White Ladies (left) is much greater than shown.

muster of all persons between the ages of sixteen and sixty to appear on 26 August in arms on Pitchcroft, a meadow just outside the city walls.

Flight from Worcester

Cromwell reached Worcester four days later and camped to the southeast of the city. After preliminary skirmishing the battle was joined in the afternoon of Wednesday 3 September and by nightfall the Royalist forces had been beaten irretrievably. Charles, admitting defeat, left the city in the early evening, and with a number of officers and a body of Scottish cavalry, slipped away towards the north.

The dejection and confusion of this moment are best reflected in Charles's own account which he dictated to Samuel Pepys some thirty years later:

Henry, Lord Wilmot, was at the Battle of Worcester. He carried out diplomatic missions for Charles in exile and was created Earl of Rochester, but did not live to see the restoration

COURTAULD INSTITUTE

After that battle was so absolutely lost, as to be beyond hope of recovery, I began to think of the best way of saving myself; and the first thought that came into my head was that, if I could possibly, I would get to London, as soon, if not sooner, than the news of our defeat could get thither; and it being near dark, I talked with some, especially with my Lord Rochester, who was then Wilmot, about their opinions, which would be the best way for me to escape, it being impossible as I thought, to get back into Scotland. I found them mightily distracted, and their opinions different of the possibility of getting into Scotland, but not one agreeing with mine, for going to London, saving my Lord Wilmot; and the truth is, I did not impart my design of going to London to any but my Lord Wilmot. But we had such a number of beaten men with us, of the horse, that I strove as soon as ever it was dark, to get from them; and though I could not get them to stand by me against the enemy, I could not get rid of them, now I had a mind to it.

So we, that is, my Lord Duke of Buckingham, Lauderdale, Derby, Wilmot, Tom Blague, Duke Darcy and several others of my servants, went along northwards towards Scotland; and at last we got about sixty that were gentlemen and officers, and slipt away out of the high-road that goes to Lancastershire, and kept on the righthand, letting all the beaten men go along the great road, and ourselves not knowing very well which way to go, for it was then too late for us to get to London, on horse-back, riding directly for it, nor could we do it, because there was yet many people of quality with us that I could not get rid of.

So we rode through a town [Stourbridge] short of Wolverhampton, betwixt that and Worcester, and went thro', there lying a troop of the enemies there that night. We rode very quietly through the town, they having nobody to watch, nor they suspecting us no more than we did them, which I learned afterwards from a country fellow.

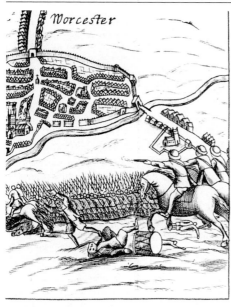

*These pictures illustrating Charles's escape accompanied a broadsheet of 1660
entitled "The HISTORY of his sacred Majesties most Wonderfull Preservation
after the Battle of Worcester"*

We went that night about twenty miles [this is clearly a mistake; the distance from Worcester to White Ladies is almost 40 miles (64km)] *to a place called White Ladys, hard by Tong-Castle, by the advice of Mr Giffard.*

This passage conveys the anxiety and excitement of this desperate journey but for some details it needs supplementing from other sources. Charles, though resolved to make for London, was forced by circumstances to alter his plans and seek shelter locally. According to accounts written in 1660, this decision was made when the party reached Kinver Heath near Kidderminster, about 18 miles (29km) north of Worcester. Daylight had gone, their guide was uncertain of the roads and the company was still too large to escape unnoticed. At some point Lord Derby had recommended Boscobel as a hiding place. He had himself sheltered there a few weeks previously and found it a quiet house in an obscure and densely wooded part of the country. At Kinver, therefore, it was resolved to make for Boscobel and one of the party, Charles Giffard, who was related to the owner of the house, was summoned to act as guide, with his servant Francis Yates.

Charles at White Ladies
However, it was to White Ladies, not to Boscobel, that Charles and his party were taken. This is explained in this way:

Upon further consideration by His Majesty and Council, and to the end the company might not know whither His Majesty directly intended, Mr Giffard was required to conduct His Majesty to some house neere Boscobel, the better to blind the design of going thither: Mr Giffard proposed White Ladies ... lying about half a mile beyond Boscobel.

It was thought too dangerous for a large number of people to know Charles's actual hiding place. Events were to prove the wisdom of this decision.

After riding through the night and arriving at White Ladies about dawn on the morning of Thursday 4 September, Charles and his companions were admitted by George Penderel, a servant of the house and one of five brothers who were to figure prominently in the events of the next few days. Frances Cotton, the owner of White Ladies, and of Boscobel too, was apparently not in residence and a boy, Bartholomew Martin, was sent to summon William Penderel, the eldest of the brothers, from Boscobel where he lived with his wife as caretaker and servant. A third brother, Richard Penderel, who lived at Hobbal Grange, a cottage about three-quarters of a mile west of White Ladies, was also sent for; and John Penderel, one of the White Ladies household, "a kind of woodward there," was roused and required to help

Richard Penderel, from a painting by Zoust, engraved by Houston

NATIONAL PORTRAIT GALLERY

His Face you see. Now breifly heare the Rest;
How well he serv'd his Prince in flight distress'.
'Twas, He whose little Houshold did Combine
In Pious Care to save: the Royall Line.
An Oake was thought most safe, for what could prove
More Luckie then the sacred tree to love
See where the Hen-roost Ladder stands; by that,
The Mighty Monarch climb'd the Boughs of State,
Where Noble Carlos lent his Manlike Knee,
The last support. of Fainting Majestie.
And Natures Tapistrie was the onely shroud
To shelter that Great Prince with Rage pursu'd

The Nutthook reaching up his Homely fare
Supply'd the want of Waiters standing Bare;
While busie Wife and Children gather wood
To dress the sheep prepar'd for Better food.
Thus many Oakes defend the British Maine
But one preserv'd the British Soveraigne.
　Pendrill thy name will shine in History
　Brighter then their's, whose Hospittallity
　Disguised Deitys hath entertayn'd
　For thine was reall tother Poets faynd.
From the very rare Print in the Possession of A.H. Sutherland Esqr.

William Penderel at the age of 84. He was the eldest and longest-lived of the brothers

A view of Boscobel House (right) with Whiteladies and the Royal Oak, by Robert Streeter. Almost certainly commissioned by Charles II in about 1670, it was recorded in the collection of James II, and hangs today at Hampton Court Palace. Charles and Richard Penderel are shown (far left) leaving White Ladies by the back way, while the rest of Charles's party gallop away from the front

Charles, according to his own account, was again advised to make for Scotland but his mind was set on reaching London, and at White Ladies he determined to make his way there on foot disguised as a countryman. He changed into "a pair of ordinary grey-cloth breeches, a lethern doublet and a green jerkin" borrowed piecemeal from the Penderels and other servants in the house. His hair was cut short, his face darkened with soot and, after the rest of his party had ridden away, he left the house on foot with Richard Penderel, and hid in a wood nearby known as Spring Coppice.

Attempt to reach Wales
Charles stayed throughout a wet September day, accompanied by Richard Penderel. According to Charles they were without food or drink, but another account says they were given a blanket for

Charles to sit on and "a mess of milk and some butter and eggs" by the wife of Francis Yates, a neighbour and relative of the Penderels (not the Francis Yates who acted as guide from Kinver to White Ladies).

During the day Charles took stock of his position:

As I was in the wood I talked with the fellow [Richard Penderel] *about getting towards London, and asking him many questions, about what gentlemen he knew; I did not find he knew any man of quality in the way towards London. And the truth is, my mind changed as I lay in the wood, and I resolved*

of another way of making my escape; which was, to get over the Severn into Wales, and so to get either to Swansey, or some of the sea-towns that I knew had commerce with France, to the end I might get over that way, as being a way that I thought none would suspect my taking; besides that, I remembered several honest gentlemen that were of my acquaintance in Wales.

So that night as soon as it was dark Richard Penderel and I took our journey on foot towards the Severn, intending to pass over a ferry half way between Bridgenorth and Shrewsbury.

As well as reflecting on his next move

Charles practised his disguise, learning from Richard a country fellow's speech and manner of walking, a "lobbing jobsons gate" as one seventeenth-century writer describes it.

On leaving the wood at nightfall Charles and Richard may have stayed for a short time at Richard's cottage, Hobbal Grange, but this is not entirely clear. Charles's narrative says that he got some bread and cheese at one of the Penderels' houses but did not go in. Other versions of this incident state that Charles went into Richard's house and met his mother, "old Goodwife Penderel." After having a meal he improved his disguise and then, with Richard, set out for Wales under the assumed name of Will Jones.

Their destination that night was a house at Madeley, 9 miles (14.5km) to the west and about 1½ miles (2.4km) from the River Severn. It was owned by a Mr Wolfe who, like the Penderels, was a Catholic and was known to Richard. It was a short journey but not without incident. Passing Evelith Mill, about 3 miles (4.8km) from Madeley, they were challenged by the miller and were forced to take to their heels down a dirty country lane and hide behind a hedge until safe from pursuit.

Arriving at Wolfe's house in the early hours of Friday 5 September, Charles learnt that the Severn crossings were closely guarded. Moreover the hiding places in the house had been discovered and were unsafe. During the day, therefore, he was forced to hide in the barn at Madeley and, since he could not cross into Wales, he resolved to walk that night to Boscobel where he hoped to hear news of Lord Wilmot and perhaps make a fresh start towards London.

Boscobel and the oak tree

On the return journey Charles and Richard waded across the stream near Evelith Mill and arrived at Boscobel at about three o'clock in the morning. Prudently Richard first approached the house alone to make sure it was safe for Charles to enter. He found hiding there one of Charles's officers from Worcester, Major William Careless, a local man who was known to the Penderels. Richard and Careless went to the wood where Charles was sheltering and took him back to the house where he was given bread and cheese and "a Posset of thin milk and small beer."

Charles did not stay long in the house but left about daybreak and, with Careless, clambered into the branches of an oak tree where the two of them hid throughout the day. This was Saturday 6 September.

The episode of the Royal Oak, as in later years it came to be known, is a crucial one in the history of Boscobel and it is worth quoting Charles's own description of this famous incident:

[Careless] *told me, that it would be very dangerous for me either to stay in that house, or to go into the wood, there being a great wood hard by Boscobel; that he knew but one way how to pass the next day, and that was, to get up into a great oak in a pretty plain place, where we might see round about us; for the enemy would certainly search all the wood for people that had made their escape. Of which proposition I approving, we (that is to say Careless and I) went, and carried up with us some victuals for the whole day, viz, bread, cheese, small bear [beer], and nothing else, and got up into a great oak, that had been lopt some three or four years before, and being grown out again, very bushy and thick, could not be seen through, and here we staid all the day.*

Memorandum, That while we were in this tree we see soldiers going up and down, in the thicket of the wood, searching for persons escaped, we seeing them, now and then, peeping out of the wood.

Other writers have little to add to this except that several accounts mention that Charles, having had little or no rest the previous two nights, slept for part of the day perched in the tree with his head in Careless's lap. Whether asleep or awake, however, they must have been extremely uncomfortable as at nightfall on their return to the house Charles is said to have declared he would rely for his future safety on the secrecy of the house rather than endure again the discomforts of the tree.

During the day the Penderel brothers had kept watch and moved about the countryside in search of news. Humphrey Penderel, the fifth of the brothers, went to Shifnal to pay taxes and while in the town was closely questioned by Commonwealth officers searching for Charles. John Penderel, who had left White Ladies on Thursday with Lord Wilmot, returned from Moseley Hall, 6 miles (9.6km) southeast of Boscobel, where he had left Wilmot in the care of its owner, Thomas Whitgreave.

On the Saturday evening at Boscobel, Charles enjoyed a greater measure of comfort than he had had since leaving Worcester. He sat down to a dish of chicken, and later he was shaved and his hair was trimmed "as short at the top as the scissors would do it, but leaving some about the ears, according to the Country mode." For his bed "a little Pallet was put in the secret place" and at night the Penderel brothers kept watch to prevent a surprise.

These details are taken from Thomas Blount's *Boscobel*, an account of Charles's escape first published in 1660. Charles is silent about the events after leaving the shelter of the tree. Indeed he telescopes the next twenty-four hours and speaks of going to Whitgreave's house at Moseley that night, that is on Saturday 6 September. But this is almost certainly wrong. All other writers, including

The Squire of Moseley, Thomas Whitgrave

Whitgreave, agree that Charles stayed at Boscobel through Saturday night and during the following day, leaving Boscobel for Moseley only on the evening of Sunday 7 September.

On the Sunday morning, we are told, Charles rose early and, "near the secret place where he lay, had the convenience of a Gallery to walk in where he was observed to spend some time in his Devotions and where he had the advantage of a window, which surveyed the Road from Tong to Brewood."

Later he came down and helped to fry mutton collops, Major Careless having gone to a neighbouring fold and secretly procured a sheep which he brought back to the house and killed. Several years later, in exile in France, Charles spoke of this episode and recalled his skill with the frying-pan at Boscobel with no little satisfaction.

❧ By the Parliament.

A PROCLAMATION

FOR THE

Difcovery and Apprehending of *CHARLS STUART*, and other Traytors
his Adherents and Abettors.

Ⱨereas CHARLS STUART Son to the late Tyrant, with divers of
the Englilh and Scotilh Nation, have lately in a Trayterous and Hoftile
maner with an Army invaded this Nation, which by the Blesſing of God
upon the Forces of this Commonwealth have been defeated, and many of
the chief Actors therein ſlain and taken priſoners; but the ſaid Charls Stuart is
eſcaped : For the ſpeedy Appꝛehending of ſuch a Malicious and Dangerous Traytoꝛ to
the Peace of this Commonwealth, The Parliament doth ſtraightly Charge and Com=
mand all Officers, as well Civil as Military, and all other the good People of this Na=
tion, That they make diligent Search and Enquiry foꝛ the ſaid Charls Stuart, and his
Abettoꝛs and Adherents in this Jnvaſion, and uſe their beſt Endeavoꝛs foꝛ the Diſco=
very and Arreſting the Bodies of them and every of them ; and being apprehended, to
bꝛing oꝛ cauſe to be bꝛought foꝛthwith and without delay, in ſafe Cuſtody befoꝛe the Par=
liament oꝛ Councel of State, to be pꝛoceeded with and oꝛdered as Juſtice ſhall require;
And if any perſon ſhall knowingly Conceal the ſaid Charls Stuart, oꝛ any his Abettoꝛs oꝛ
Adherents, oꝛ ſhall not Reveal the Places of their Abode oꝛ Being, if it be in their
power ſo to do, The Parliament doth Declare, That they will hold them as partakers
and Abettoꝛs of their Trayterous and Wicked Pꝛactices and Deſigns : And the Parlia=
ment doth further Publiſh and Declare, That whoſoever ſhall appꝛehend the perſon of
the ſaid Charls Stuart, and ſhall bꝛing oꝛ cauſe him to be bꝛought to the Parliament oꝛ Coun=
cel of State, ſhall have given and beſtowed on him oꝛ them as a Reward foꝛ ſuch Ser=
vice, the ſum of One thouſand pounds ; And all Officers, Civil and Military, are requi=
red to be aiding and aſsiſting unto ſuch perſon and perſons therein.   Given at Weſtminſter
this Tenth day of September, One thouſand ſix hundꝛed fifty one.

Wednefday the Tenth of September. 1651.

Rdered by the Parliament, That this Proclamation be forthwith Printed and Publiſhed.

Hen: Scobell, *Cleric. Parliamenti.*

London, Printed by *John Field*, Printer to the Parliament of *England.* 1651.

*A proclaimation issued on 10 September 1651, "for the discovery and
apprehending of Charles Stuart, and other traitors his adherents and
abettors." By then Charles was on his way to Bristol*

The rest of the day he spent in or near the house and part of it in a "pretty Arbor in Boscobel garden, which grew upon a Mount and wherein there was a Stone Table and Seats about it."

Some descriptions tend to give much too peaceful a picture of this Sunday at Boscobel. Refreshed by his rest and the more substantial food, with the memories of Worcester less overwhelming, and encouraged perhaps by his success so far in evading capture, Charles was probably more hopeful, but his position was still perilous and his future uncertain. On the Sunday morning John Penderel was sent to Moseley to seek the help of Lord Wilmot and, coming upon Whitgreave, the owner of Moseley, and Father Huddleston, a Catholic priest who was residing with Whitgreave, John described Charles as "much dejected, having no hopes or prospect of redress."

Journey to Bristol

Lord Wilmot was not at Moseley, having moved the previous night to Colonel Lane's house, Bentley Hall, 5 miles (8km) away, with the intention of travelling with the Colonel's sister, Mistress Jane Lane, to Bristol. Whitgreave and Huddleston took John Penderel to Bentley and there it was arranged that Wilmot should return that night to Moseley to await Charles, who would be brought from Boscobel by the Penderels.

On the Sunday evening, therefore, four days after his defeat at Worcester, Charles left Boscobel accompanied by the five Penderels and their brother-in-law Francis Yates to cover the few miles to Moseley. His feet were sore and chafed after his walk to and from Madeley, so for part of the journey he rode on Humphrey Penderel's mill-horse. This has given rise to the delightful but perhaps apocryphal story of Charles complaining that it was "the Heaviest Dull Jade he ever rode on,"

Jane Lane, with whom Charles travelled to Bristol disguised as a servant. After the news of the King's escape became public in October 1651, she and her brother Colonel John Lane fled in disguise and were welcomed in Paris by Charles. At the Restoration both were rewarded for their services

to which Humphrey replied, "My liege! can you blame the horse to go heavily, when he has the weight of three Kingdoms on his back?"

Charles and his escort arrived at Moseley in the early hours of Monday morning, 8 September, and here the story as it affects Boscobel, White Ladies and the Penderels ends. Charles stayed at Moseley for two days and after spending a few hours at Bentley set off for Bristol early on Wednesday 10 September, dressed as a serving man and riding with Mistress Lane. From Bristol he made his way eventually through a series of adventures to Brighthelmeston (Brighton) and on the morning of 15 October 1651, he sailed secretly from a creek near Shoreham in the coal brig *Surprise* to seek

NATIONAL PORTRAIT GALLERY

Charles in disguise, riding with Jane Lane. A servant is behind them and Lord Wilmot is in the distance

shelter in France, remaining in exile until 1660.

Aftermath

Boscobel and White Ladies were searched shortly after Charles had departed and the Penderels were closely questioned. Francis Yates, Charles's guide from Kinver to White Ladies, was executed in Oxford for his part in the affair, but, perhaps rather surprisingly, no harm came to any of Charles's other helpers. An inaccurate account of Charles's escape appeared in print in November 1651, mentioning a hollow tree, a countryman's disguise and the help of a lady, but the full story was not made public until the Restoration when the principal figures were received by Charles at his Court in Whitehall and duly rewarded for their services. The Penderels received pensions which were granted to them and their descendants in perpetuity and which are paid to this day.

William, the eldest of the five brothers, continued to live at Boscobel until his death in 1700 and was followed there by his descendants who were living in the house during the eighteenth century. John and Humphrey both died before him, in

the 1680s, and so did Richard, "Trusty Dick," who came to live in London and was buried in February 1671 in the churchyard of St Giles-in-the-Fields, Holborn, where his monument may still be seen. The tomb, much repaired and restored, is in the churchyard southeast of the church but the stone slab, with its inscription, which once formed the top of the tomb was moved in 1922 and placed in the south porch of the church.

As for Boscobel and the Royal Oak, their fame spread rapidly on Charles's return in 1660, and if the house itself was little changed the tree soon suffered from the attentions of an enthusiastic public (see page 27). Its story caught the imagination, as indeed it does today, and to commemorate its name a new order of chivalry was proposed, the Knights of the Royal Oak, whose members would be distinguished for their loyalty. This idea was not pursued for fear it would "keep awake animosities which it was the part of wisdom to lull to sleep," but each year on 29 May, the birthday of Charles II, the Royal Oak is remembered on Oak Apple Day, while countless inn signs throughout the country still remind one of this celebrated tree.

Tour of Boscobel House

ENGLISH HERITAGE/SKYSCAN

Looking north over Boscobel House. The garden is on the right and the farmyard top left. See the plan on page 18

It is not known exactly when Boscobel was built. The oldest part is the north range, timber framed and two storeyed (**7** on the plan on page 18). At right angles to this is the main body of the house **6** which was probably built about 1630 by John Giffard, eldest son of Edward Giffard of White Ladies, who was himself descended from the Giffards of Chillington. Blount, writing in 1660, speaks of it as having been built "about 30 years before."

The name Boscobel is interesting and, if we may trust Blount again, derives from the complimentary remarks of one of John Giffard's friends. According to Blount, Giffard invited "friends and neighbours to a house-warming feast and desiring Sir Basil Brook (of Madeley) to give the house a name he aptly called it Boscobel

from the Italian Bosco Bello, because it is seated in the midst of fair woods."

Its remote position in an area of dense woodland, as it was in the seventeenth century, was providential as far as Charles was concerned and it may also explain the nature of the building itself. It is more a lodge than a house, intended for the occasional use of the owner and his guests rather than as a permanent residence. No doubt it served several needs, including perhaps accommodating Giffard and his guests when out hunting. By tradition part of its purpose was to serve in times of need as a secret shelter for Roman priests, the Giffards themselves being a Catholic family.

On the death of John Giffard both White Ladies and Boscobel passed to his

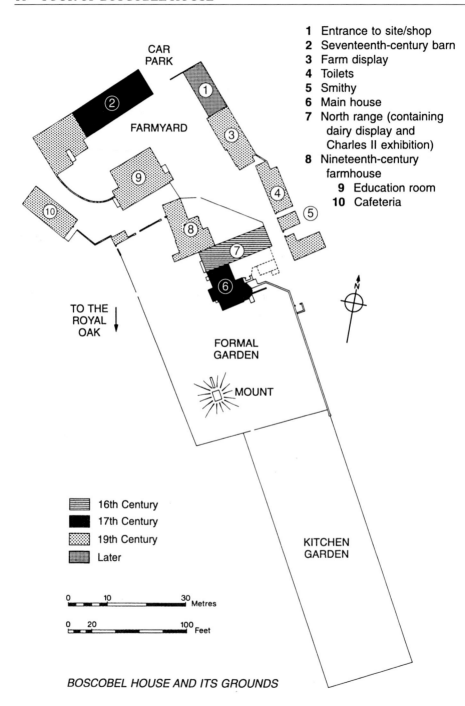

1 Entrance to site/shop
2 Seventeenth-century barn
3 Farm display
4 Toilets
5 Smithy
6 Main house
7 North range (containing dairy display and Charles II exhibition)
8 Nineteenth-century farmhouse
9 Education room
10 Cafeteria

CAR PARK

FARMYARD

TO THE ROYAL OAK

FORMAL GARDEN

MOUNT

KITCHEN GARDEN

16th Century
17th Century
19th Century
Later

0   10   30 Metres
0   20   100 Feet

BOSCOBEL HOUSE AND ITS GROUNDS

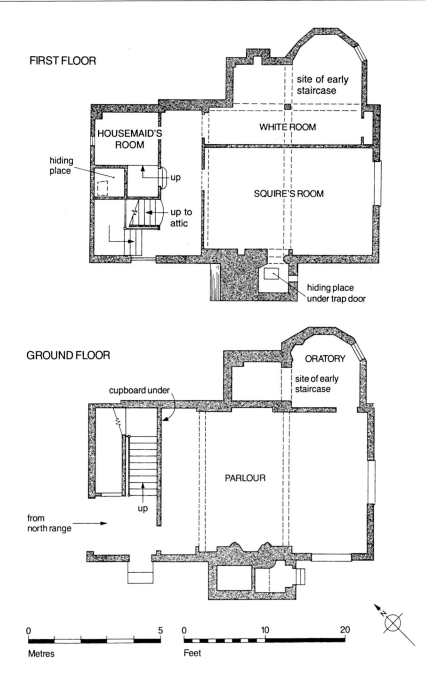

FIRST FLOOR

site of early staircase

HOUSEMAID'S ROOM

WHITE ROOM

hiding place

up

up to attic

SQUIRE'S ROOM

hiding place under trap door

GROUND FLOOR

ORATORY

cupboard under

site of early staircase

PARLOUR

up

from north range

0   5

Metres

0   10   20

Feet

PLAN OF THE MAIN PART OF BOSCOBEL HOUSE

Boscobel House seen across the farmyard

daughter, Frances, who in 1633 had married John Cotton of Gedding Abbots, Huntingdonshire. In 1651 the two houses were still in the possession of Frances Cotton, by this time a widow, but shortly afterwards they passed to Basil Fitzherbert of Norbury and Swynnerton who had married Jane Cotton, Frances's only daughter, in 1648. They remained in Fitzherbert ownership, being let to a succession of tenants including descendants of the Penderels, until 1812 when Boscobel and the greater part of the White Ladies estate, but not the site of White Ladies itself, was sold to Walter Evans of Darley in Derbyshire.

Boscobel remained in the Evans family during the nineteenth century and while in their ownership both house and gardens were restored in an attempt to re-create their appearance in Charles II's day - a story that is told in more detail on page 30. In 1918 the estate was bought by the Earl of Bradford who in 1954 placed the house and the tree in the guardianship of the Ministry of Works. Since 1984 it has been in the care of English Heritage, which has refurnished the house to resemble its nineteenth-century appearance.

TOUR

The present approach to the house is across a **farmyard.** On the far (north) side is a large seventeenth-century timber-framed barn **2.** However, most of the

The Parlour

buildings around the yard are nineteenth-century in date: to your left, beyond the shop, the large open-fronted farm building **3** contains a display of farm machinery, while beyond the lavatories is the former smithy **5**.

Entrance to the house is through the nineteenth-century **farmhouse 8.** Painted on the outside in black and white to simulate timber framing, its walls are in fact entirely of brick. Next to this is the **north range 7,** the oldest part of Boscobel House. In the days of the working farm its ground floor was used as a dairy, and cheese- and butter-making implements are now displayed here. At the time of Charles's stay at Boscobel, however, it probably contained the kitchen, other service rooms, and accommodation for William Penderel and his wife, the servants of the house. It is not all of the same date, as can be seen from the differences in the timber framing.

The first floor of the north range now contains an exhibition telling the story of Charles's escape after the Battle of Worcester.

Ground floor

Moving from the waiting area and into the north range, you enter the room used as the **Hall** during the nineteenth century. The family would have entered here after approaching Boscobel on the carriage drive to the east of the barn and stables.

From here you enter the main body of the house, past a nineteenth-century staircase which has had its original decorative scheme restored, and into the **Parlour.** Its walls are panelled and above the panelling is a plaster frieze with a continuous interlacing pattern. This is a plausible piece of period decoration using Jacobean motifs, but during the course of repair fragments of earlier plasterwork were discovered underneath it, revealing it to be a later alteration. Though parts of the panelling are Jacobean, this too shows signs of alteration, particularly around the windows which are glazed in a manner typical of the early nineteenth century.

The panels of black marble immediately above the fireplace have three designs engraved on their surfaces. These are, from left to right, a view of Boscobel with two figures in the foreground, presumably intended to represent Charles II and Richard Penderel; a view of Charles hiding in the oak with soldiers searching round the tree; and a scene of Charles on the way to Moseley escorted by the Penderels and Francis Yates. Two of these engravings were designed by Mrs Edmund Carr, one of the daughters of Walter Evans, and the third is based on an engraving in Blount's *Boscobel.*

The fireplace was installed in the nineteenth century but the elaborate arcaded panelling with carved ornament over the fireplace is possibly Jacobean, though not in its original position.

The room as we see it now owes much to the restoration carried out by the Evans family in the nineteenth century, but in the seventeenth century its character was probably very similar. At that time it was also the principal living room in the house. King Charles was said to have dined at a long oak table in this room, and the table which left the house in 1918 was described as having survived from that time. It was very similar to the table which is here now. A portrait of Charles after the Restoration hangs above the table, while a portrait of Oliver Cromwell hangs at the other end. The oak graining on the frieze and beams is a recreation of the

The Oratory. The portrait above the fireplace is of Jane Penderel or "Dame Joan," the wife of William Penderel

Oliver Cromwell

decoration which was found beneath recent white limewash.

A door leads from the far end of the room into a small chamber known since the late nineteenth century as the **Oratory** (see page 22). Before the nineteenth-century changes it was probably the position of the original staircase. The walls here are painted to simulate panelling.

A small oak chest, inscribed 1652, is carved with scenes of Charles's escape from Worcester to Boscobel. Although some pieces of the chest may be contemporary with Charles's time, the carved decoration is nineteenth-century in date. The chest was first noted in the Oratory in 1885, but left the house before the sale of the contents in 1918. It has recently been returned by a descendant of the Evans family.

First floor

On the upper floor the main chamber,

known as the **Squire's Room** in the nineteenth century, is panelled but, as in the Parlour below, the panelling bears many signs of alteration. The oak graining on the frieze and beams belongs to the Evans period, and was exposed when the white limewash was removed in 1988. Seventeenth-century engravings show a window in this room in the west wall, to the left of the fireplace, and alterations in the panelling indicate its possible position. Also in the west wall is a small fireplace with a surround of delft tiles, and immediately to the left of this is a door which opens into a small chamber or closet contained in the thickness of the chimney stack. Under the floor of this closet is one of the Boscobel "secret places," a small space of the same area as the closet but only 2 feet 3 inches (686mm) high. It has no window or window slit and no visible means of access other than through the upper floor, although it is said that at one time it was possible to slip through into the space below.

Secret places, priest holes and hiding places of various sorts are not uncommon features of buildings of the sixteenth and seventeenth centuries. Some are convincing, some are obviously spurious. Very few indeed can be established with any certainty. Boscobel has two such secret places - that described above is the less convincing. The second is found in the attic (see page 24).

It is true that chimney stacks were frequently used to provide places of concealment but, as they were obvious places to be searched, much skill and ingenuity were needed if the hiding places were to be effective. At Boscobel this is hardly the case. The small door at the base of the stack, an early feature, is the reverse of secret. It advertises the cavities in the stack and if there was indeed access to the space above, discovery was almost

The White Room

invited. There must be doubt about the effectiveness of this hiding place, or indeed whether it was a hiding place at all. It is more likely that this space in the stack was originally used as an earth closet or privy and the small door at the base of the stack was for the purpose of cleaning the bottom of the shaft. If so, the present hiding place is the creation of some later owner or tenant adapting a utilitarian feature to a more romantic role.

The second chamber, the **White Room,** on the east side of the house, was so called during the nineteenth century because the panelling was painted white and the bed was hung with white dimity bedhangings. These have been recreated on a similar bed. The room is irregular in shape and has a free-standing oak post in the centre of the floor which is part of the timber-framed structure of the house. It is partly panelled and has a decorated plaster frieze and, over the small fireplace in the east wall, four small plaques, two of them with tiny busts in low relief.

In the seventeenth century there was probably just one large chamber on this floor, extending as far as the oak post. The second chamber is a nineteenth-century alteration made when more bedrooms were needed. To create an extra room the principal chamber was reduced in size, a small extension built with a fireplace, and the old staircase removed to gain additional space.

Attic

On the attic landing, next to the Squire's Room and White Room, are two doors, one leading into a housemaid's cupboard at a slightly higher level, and one opening on to the attic stairs. At the head of these stairs is a small trap door which gives access to the second of the two secret places of the house, a slightly larger space than the first but still only 4 feet by 3 feet 4 inches (1.2 by 1m) across and just over 4 feet (1.2m) high.

Here Charles is said to have spent the night when he stayed in the house; and the "gallery" he is described as walking in, the following morning, has been interpreted as the attic which runs the length of the house and from which one can indeed survey the road from Tong to Brewood. The early accounts of Charles's escape, however, though mentioning a secret place do not describe exactly where it lay. The first detailed description of a hiding place is given by the antiquary William Stukeley who visited the house in 1712. Stukeley states that the house was then occupied by the grand-daughter of William Penderel and he continues: "the floor of the garret (which is a popish chapel) being matted prevents any suspicion of a little cavity with a trap door over the staircase, where the king hid; his bed was artfully placed behind some wainscot that shut up very close:" This description could be applied to the hiding place one sees now. There are signs of alteration but in essentials it may well represent the cramped and awkward space that Charles used for his night's lodging. It could indeed be said of it that "his dormitory (was) none of the best, nor his bed the easiest."

Stairs to the attic

The attic and the **Bower Room** beyond were used as bedrooms during the nineteenth century. A small spinning wheel, which was said to be Dame Penderel's, was displayed here in the nineteenth century, but the large example now in its place was brought into the house by the Earl of Bradford after the original was sold in 1918.

Garden and exterior

Seventeenth-century views of Boscobel show a garden south and west of the house laid out in small formal beds edged with box, and the present garden follows a similar pattern. The mount still stands in the southwest corner in the position shown on early engravings but the arbour on the mount no longer survives. It was probably an insubstantial structure covered with climbing shrubs, such as a

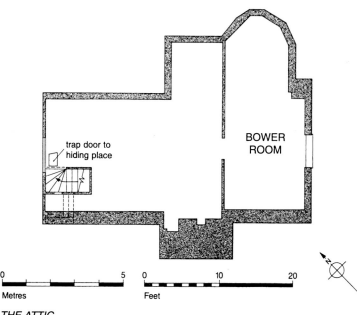

trap door to
hiding place

BOWER
ROOM

0 ——————— 5   0 ————————— 10 ————————— 20

Metres   Feet

THE ATTIC

Boscobel House from the south

visitor to Boscobel saw at the end of the eighteenth century. The present timber shelter on the top of the mount is modern.

Looking back at the house from the garden and comparing it with seventeenth-century views (see, for example, pages 5 and 11), the alterations are plain to see. The windows have been changed, the roof altered, and the upper part of the chimney stack rebuilt. Most strikingly, whereas in the seventeenth century its framing was exposed, giving the house the half-timbered appearance typical of older buildings in Shropshire and neighbouring counties, its walls are now covered with stucco, a dress that is plain and monotonous compared with its original appearance. The stucco was applied at quite an early date, certainly by the end of the eighteenth century, probably to disguise the fact that parts of the timber framing had decayed and were

being replaced with brick.

One curious feature of the exterior occurs on the outer face of the chimney stack, where there are five marks on the plaster simulating windows and window slits. These have a long history. They are shown on seventeenth-century engravings and appear again on paintings of the house in the late eighteenth century. Early engravings also depict the small door on the south side of the stack and a flight of steps rising to it. This door leads into a narrow space contrived in the thickness of the stack which is reputed to have had access at one time to the "secret place" immediately above (see page 23).

Despite all the changes, the house still stands in size and shape very much as it was in 1651. It has escaped major extension and rebuilding and its survival gives it a special importance in the story of Charles's escape.

The Royal Oak

The tree today, with Boscobel House in the distance

Southwest of the house, at a distance of about 150 yards (137m) and surrounded by an iron paling, is the tree known as the Royal Oak. There is some doubt whether this is in fact the Royal Oak or a younger tree which has taken its place and name. Let us look briefly at its history.

Immediately the story of Boscobel became known, people flocked to see the house and the oak. Very soon the tree was injured by souvenir hunters removing its young boughs. The damage was so great that before 1680 the then owners of Boscobel, Basil and Jane Fitzherbert, were forced to crop part of the tree and protect it with a high brick wall. Over a door in

the wall they placed a stone tablet carved with an inscription reciting the fame and history of the tree.

Their action may have been too late to save the tree or there may have been further damage in later years, one cannot say, but in 1706 John Evelyn wrote that he had heard that the "Famous Oak near White Ladys" had been killed by people hacking the boughs and bark, and six years later William Stukeley described the tree as "almost cut away by travellers." He also remarked that "a young thriving plant from one of its acorns" was growing "close by the side."

This is the first record of a younger tree

The oak, surrounded by the wall that was built to protect it, from the "Gentleman's Magazine" of 1809

growing near the old oak, but during the eighteenth century there are several other accounts of two trees, the one decayed, the other growing beside it, until towards the end of the century a change occurs, the older tree is no longer mentioned and the younger tree alone figures in the descriptions.

In 1784 there is a careful account of the surrounding brick wall, by this time neglected and ruinous, and of the stone tablet with its inscription, but within the enclosure only one tree is described, a tree of middling size, growing within the wall but not in the centre. Again in 1791 only one tree is referred to, a tree of "about four score years old," and in 1809 a writer who had visited Boscobel two years earlier speaks of a tree "fine and thrifty ... said to have originated from an acorn of the old Oak."

None of these writers mentions a second tree, nor even the remains of one. They speak of the tree they saw as a relatively young one and do not claim that it was the original oak.

Indeed the writer of 1784 also remarks that "the old tree has been carried away piece-meal by curious visitors" and adds that "many snuff-boxes and other toys have been made from the wood of this famous oak." The passion for souvenirs, first noted by Thomas Blount in 1660, had evidently continued unabated. Snuff-boxes, tobacco-stoppers and other similar items were fashioned from wood taken from the tree, and not even its roots were spared. In the early nineteenth century a seat is mentioned, "a large block with an inscription," cut from part of the root of the Royal Oak!

There is also some evidence of how the tree was finally destroyed. It comes from the Reverend Joseph Dale, curate of Donington from 1811 to 1849, who wrote that some old people at the beginning of the nineteenth century had told him that the last remains of the Royal Oak had been rooted up many years before, and the position of the younger tree in a corner of the enclosure had made it possible to take out "the whole of the stock and the thickest portion of the roots" of the old oak.

It is difficult to resist the conclusion that by the end of the eighteenth century the Royal Oak no longer survived. Within the enclosure a younger tree had taken root and grown, and it is this tree that stands at Boscobel today, a memorial to the old oak and, if Stukeley is correct, a descendant of the original tree.

Within the present enclosure are three brass plates engraved with commem-orative inscriptions. Two are in Latin and one in English. The smallest plate is the one provided by Basil and Eliza Fitzherbert in 1787 when they rebuilt the brick wall of their predecessors, Basil and Jane Fitzherbert. The original stone tablet with its inscription had by this time been damaged or destroyed.

The two larger brass plates were placed here by Miss Elizabeth Evans in 1875. They give a history of the tree and describe how the second brick wall was replaced in 1817 by iron railings erected by Miss Frances Evans. The inscription also refers to the tree as the original Royal Oak. These later plates took the place of yet another made in 1845 which described the tree as being descended from the Royal Oak.

Between 1845 and 1875, therefore, opinion changed and it may seem strange that there should be this sudden alteration. But by 1875 the second tree had grown to a considerable size; also the memory of an earlier tree had faded from men's minds and eye-witnesses of an older stump no longer lived to tell the tale. Perhaps even more important, the climate of opinion had changed. Harrison Ainsworth's romance, *Boscobel, or the Royal Oak*, had appeared in 1872 and literature about Charles II's adventures was much in demand. It was at this time that the inscription was altered, and one feels that of all the reasons for the change sentiment played the major part.

Trees descended from the Boscobel oak no doubt flourish in many parts of the country. There is indeed a pleasant tradition that after his restoration King Charles II planted Boscobel acorns in St James's Park and carefully watered them himself. In fact a gardeners' dictionary of 1759 mentions a sapling raised from a Boscobel acorn growing near St James's Palace. It adds, however, that it was cut down at a quite early date, probably when Marlborough House was built.

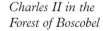

Charles II in the Forest of Boscobel

The Romantic Idea of Boscobel

Boscobel when it was in use as a farm, in about 1910

In the early seventeenth century the chase - stag-hunting on horseback - was a courtly activity, with associations of chivalry and privilege, and John Giffard's remote hunting lodge, tall, gabled and elaborately framed, was from the first a consciously romantic building. It cannot be an accident that the name recalls the medieval tradition by which castles and abbeys were given such names at Beaumont, Beaulieu, Belvoir and Beaumaris.

With the restoration of the monarchy in 1660 the story of the King's escape from Worcester became widely known, several accounts of it - many of them fanciful - appearing within months of his return to London. The episode which most captured the public imagination was his concealment in the tree at Boscobel,

partly because it was an attractive and heroic story, but also because of its symbolism. Oaks were already associated with the idea of royalty. Evelyn records in his *Numismata* a medal, struck in 1638 to commemorate the investiture of Charles as Prince of Wales, showing an oak tree overshadowing its sapling as a symbol of the royal succession. By 1662 hundreds of people had flocked to Boscobel "chiefly to behold the Royal oake," and snuff boxes and other toys made from its wood became popular relics.

Although the Protestant revolution of 1689 forced James II from the throne, the story of his brother's escape and concealment at Boscobel continued to attract interest. The King's own account of his escape, which he had related to the diarist Pepys in 1680, was first published in 1766 and was reprinted several times over the following forty years. It was perhaps inevitable that with the resurgence of romantic feeling at the end of the eighteenth century Boscobel would again acquire the status of a shrine.

By the end of the eighteenth century the house had been rendered with plaster, making it weatherproof but concealing the frame and destroying much of its character. The gardens shown in seventeenth-century illustrations had disappeared and there was only "a pretty little kitchen-garden planted with nut-hedges, currant and gooseberry bushes." Although the tenants had "always shown a proper attention to every curious stranger, and a kind hospitality within-doors when a politeness of behaviour entitled those strangers to such a distinction," it is clear that the farm was a working farm, visitors were few, and the buildings and gardens were maintained for their practical utility with little regard for their sentimental value.

It was no doubt the romantic association of the place that led Walter Evans to buy the White Ladies estate in 1812, for the alterations he made to the house for his step daughter Frances were designed to recapture as much as possible of its historic character. Frances's elder sister Elizabeth later wrote that her step father "wished to restore the appearance of the place to what it was when Charles was there, and took the old prints of the place for a pattern." The work was picturesque rather than scholarly. Render and brickwork were painted to resemble timber framing, sash windows with traceried glazing replaced unfashionable but authentic casements and an eighteenth-century Gothick chimneypiece was bought and put into the dining room, its overmantel decorated (at the suggestion of Mrs Evans) with scenes of the King's escape. The garden was redesigned in imitation of a seventeenth-century parterre and the arbour referred to in old accounts was reconstructed. A commemorative pebble inscription was laid by the youngest sister, Ellen: "She was not much above twenty, and much enjoyed the work." By 1824 Boscobel was being described as "nearly in its original state, but some parts have been much

The attic, showing the hatch to the hiding place open beside the stairs. A similar view was photographed for use as a postcard in about 1900

changed." So strong was the sense of the divinity of kingship that the upper hiding place, reached by a trap door from the attic, was known without irony as the "sacred hole."

Elizabeth Evans, to whom the property passed in 1873, spent a month at Boscobel every summer, but for most of the year the tenant farmer seems to have been able to show the old parts of the house to the public. Despite its title, the first guidebook to the house was George Dodd's *Narrative of the Adventure of Charles the Second*, of which the second edition was published in 1859. Regular opening hours are first recorded in 1870, and in 1871 Steen and Blacket's *Original Illustrated Wolverhampton Guide* advised visitors that Boscobel was "about two miles distant from the village of Albrighton ... which may be reached by various trains during the day, per the Great Western Railway."

The popular appeal of the story of the King's escape from Worcester had been confirmed by the success of two novels, *Brambletye House* by Horatio Smith and *Woodstock* by Sir Walter Scott, both of which appeared in 1826. Although set in 1651, the adventures they told were wholly imaginary, being as loosely based on historical events as Walter Evans's restoration of the house was on genuine seventeenth-century building. A generation later, historical fiction, like architecture, had become much more archaeological in its approach. Another popular novelist, William Harrison Ainsworth, much influenced by Scott but determined to be more "correct," wrote a further account of the escape, as fictional in detail as Scott's but far more closely based on recorded events and set in identifiable surroundings. *Boscobel, or the Royal Oak* first appeared in the *New Monthly Magazine* in 1872 and quickly went through two editions. Its effect on

the house may be judged by taking a passage, which needless to say was entirely invented by Ainsworth, in which the King is told that one of the rooms is an oratory:

"I see no altar," observed Charles.
William Penderel opened a recess in the wall, so contrived that it had quite escaped the King's attention, and disclosed a small altar with a cross above it.
"Here we pay our devotions in private," he said.
"And here I will pay mine," rejoined Charles.

Ainsworth set this scene in the small room which opens off the dining room, and in 1877 - only five years after *Boscobel* was published - a guidebook appeared which stated as a historical fact that this was "formerly an oratory ... a small altar, surmounted by a crucifix was hidden in a secret recess within the wall." Later guides repeated the same story, and by 1913 the room was known as the Oratory and had been fitted up with a reproduction altarpiece. Similarly, in 1875 Miss Evans, being "persuaded ... that the present tree is the one which sheltered King Charles II," removed the words *"qua ex arbore quercum hac, uti fetur, ortam. . ."* (this oak, descended, it is said, from the tree ...) from the inscription put up by her sister. When the British Archaeological Association visited Boscobel, Ainsworth acted as guide and read as his paper a passage from his novel "good humouredly urging ... that as the historic interest of the place was of so romantic a character, there could he thought be no objection to the romantic colour which he had imparted to the relation of its story."

The idea of Boscobel even crossed the Atlantic, "the poetic outlines of Boscobel towers" being translated to the banks of the Hudson in an American novel of the 1880s. In this version the park kept its "ancestral trees," the name Boscobel its genuine etymology - except that the language from which it derived was said to be Indian rather than Italian. Boscobel had entered the imagination even though the events that happened there in September 1651 had been forgotten. In the years before the First World War, Boscobel became "a sort of Mecca for Black Country trippers," schoolchildren walked from Wolverhampton when they had a day's holiday and guests staying at nearby country houses were brought to see the place where the King had been concealed. Disraeli came when he was staying with the Earl of Bradford at Weston Park in 1873, Lord Salisbury in 1883 and the future Queen Mary in 1889.

The house was offered for sale in 1913, and the contents assembled by the Evans family were dispersed. It was eventually purchased by Lord Bradford, who partly refurnished it and reopened it to the public. The hunting lodge was placed in the guardianship of the Ministry of Works in 1954, and the rest of the farm buildings were acquired in 1967. Part of the house (probably an extension built by Walter Evans in the early nineteenth century) was demolished by the Ministry, which also opened up part of the timber frame of the sixteenth-century range to display the original form of its construction.

Boscobel has been in the care of English Heritage since 1984. It has been refurnished and its internal decoration has been restored to its appearance when it was first opened to the public in the nineteenth century. A collection of farm implements is displayed in the barn to give an impression of what the farmyard may have looked like at around the same time.

The Dining Room

White Ladies Priory

*Detail from Robert Streeter's painting showing the house at White Ladies in the
seventeenth century to have been a substantial building with a two-storeyed
entrance porch, a large hall probably open to the roof, and a range of chambers at
the west end of the hall. In front of the house was a walled courtyard guarded by a
small timber-framed gatehouse which stood opposite the entrance porch*

It was to White Ladies that Charles was
first taken after fleeing from Worcester.
Then it was a large, timber-framed house
built on the site of a medieval nunnery
and incorporating some of the nunnery
buildings. The house has now gone, but
on the site are the remains of the medieval
church of the nunnery and some
interesting grave slabs.

History of the priory
The Priory of St Leonard at Brewood,
generally called White Ladies, was
founded towards the end of the twelfth
century for nuns or canonesses of the
Order of St Augustine. These nuns were
governed by the Rule of St Augustine of
Hippo, which laid down guidelines for the
maintenance of a communal religious life.

Less exacting than the Benedictine Rule, which formed the basis of the more rigorous monastic communities, it enabled its followers to perform duties within the church and parish outside the priory itself.

The endowment of White Ladies was modest and, apart from its main property at Brewood, consisted mostly of scattered parcels of land in a triangular area now bounded by Shifnal on the west, Wolverhampton on the southeast, and Bridgnorth on the southwest, although it, also had isolated holdings in west Shropshire and in Nottinghamshire. Consequently, the convent was small, its numbers varying between five and nine nuns in the later Middle Ages.

The little that is known of the history of the house is uneventful, the convent living quietly on the modest rents it received from its property. The only complaints against it were minor ones, as in 1338 when there was some evidence of expenditure on luxuries and it was said that the convent kept hounds.

At the valuation of monastic property in 1535 White Ladies was assessed as having a clear annual value of little more than £17, and it therefore fell within the scope of the Act of 1536 by which monasteries of less than £200 annual value were to be closed. Lord Stafford was anxious to acquire the property, but when in the spring of 1537 a royal official produced letters for its disposal the price asked was more than anyone was willing to pay. There were still four nuns in the house a year later, but by May 1538 the dispersal of the convent was complete and the site was leased to William Skevington of Wolverhampton for a term of twenty-one years.

Since the time of Leland, the King's Antiquary, who visited White Ladies shortly after it was dissolved, the house has often been referred to as having belonged to the Cistercian Order. This was due to a confusion between the dress of Cistercian and Augustinian nuns, who both wore white. The true style and title is given in the fourteenth-century registers of the Bishops of Hereford as "the prioress and convent of White nuns of St Leonard of Brewood, of the Order of St Augustine."

Priory church

The domestic buildings of the priory and the sixteenth-century house that partly replaced them have long since been destroyed, and all that remains today are the ruins of the priory church and the nineteenth-century boundary wall of the small graveyard that was formed in the church and to the south of it.

The ruins, however, form an admirable example of a small priory church, little altered since it was first built at the end of the twelfth century. It consisted of a square-ended aisleless presbytery, the eastern arm containing the main altar, of three bays or divisions. There were simple north and south transepts or side arms, apparently without the usual chapels on the east wall, and an aisleless nave - the main body of the church - with five bays. Only the north wall of the **presbytery** remains, but most of this stands to its full height, as can be seen from the fragments of the external row of stone brackets (corbels) to take the eaves of the roof. There was a plain round-headed window in each bay, the two western ones surviving intact. Between the central and eastern bays there are the remains of a round-headed cupboard on the inside face of the wall.

Beneath the central window a doorway, of which the jambs (side posts) remain, was inserted later in the Middle Ages leading to a building which was added in the angle between the presbytery and the north transept. This building was probably a sacristy, where sacred vessels

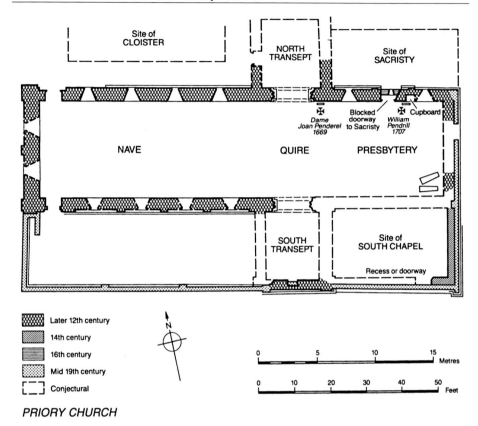

PRIORY CHURCH

and vestments were kept, but it has left no traces of its presence except this doorway and the beam holes for its roof cut into the external facework of the presbytery wall. When the sacristy was demolished after the Dissolution, the doorway was walled up and a small rectangular window was made in the blocking.

The nineteenth-century graveyard wall can be seen standing on the foundation of the square east end of the medieval presbytery, of which the lower part of the plinth or projecting base course can be recognised in places. Foundations also exist beneath the southern part of the graveyard wall, with one stone of the jamb

of a doorway or recess near its southeast angle, all showing that an addition was made on this side of the presbytery similar to the sacristy on the other side, but possibly serving as a chapel.

The fine round-headed arch leading into the **north transept** is intact and the capitals at the heads of the columns to either side have an interesting variety of designs, all still in the Romanesque tradition of architecture characteristic of the twelfth century. Little else remains of this transept, although the extent of its foundations has been marked out on the grass, but there is just enough left of its west wall to show a fragment of string course, a horizontal band of masonry which probably continued to this point from the hoodmould of a doorway that may have existed further north in the wall. A doorway in this position is commonly found in monastic churches that have no aisles to their naves, and it would serve as the eastern processional way from the church to the cloister; the hoodmould or dripstone protected the head of the door from rain.

Only the lower part of the south wall of the **south transept** is left, with the remains of a window and a blocked recess beneath.

Each bay of the **nave** had a window in both north and south walls, the northern ones being well preserved. The bays are marked externally by pilaster buttresses - masonry supports in the form of flat columns attached to the wall - on the south wall only, because of the presence of the cloister against the north wall. The westernmost bay also has a doorway in both north and south walls, the former with an interesting moulding round its head of a type common in western France but rare in England; a few stones of the head and one of the caps that support it are modern replacements. The west wall has two windows but no doorway.

Convent buildings and later house

The cloister and domestic buildings lay to the north of the church, but no trace of them remains and it is quite likely that they were of timber-framed construction.

A seventeenth-century painting by Robert Streeter (see page 34) shows a walled garden south of the priory church with a doorway in its south wall and minor buildings along its west side. This may well have been the outer court of the priory, with access for lay people to the church through the south doorway of the nave. The position of the timber-framed house in this view also suggests that it may

have grown out of the former lodging of the prioress in a wing projecting from the west range of the cloister buildings, a position favoured for such lodgings in some other religious houses.

In this house Charles and his party found shelter in the early hours of Thursday 4 September, and here the first preparations were made for his escape. No trace of it now survives, and for evidence as to its appearance we have to rely on Streeter's painting.

Little is known of the history of the building. Although ownership of the property had been granted in 1540 to William Whorwood, Henry VIII's Solicitor General, the house may well have been built by William Skevington who had obtained a lease of the priory in 1538 and who was buried at Tong in 1550. Later, White Ladies passed to Edward Giffard, whose first wife was William Skevington's widow, Joan. From Edward Giffard it passed to his son John (see page 17), and afterwards followed the descent of Boscobel until 1812. During the eighteenth century the house was entirely demolished except for the gatehouse which was still standing in 1809, used as a labourer's cottage. In 1812, when Boscobel and much of the White Ladies estate was sold, the site of the priory remained in the ownership of the Fitzherbert family. In 1938 it was placed by Lord Stafford in the guardianship of the Office of Works.

Gravestones

Until 1844 the church was used as a burial place for Roman Catholics, and a number of gravestones have been found on the site, some placed against the walls of the church. The most interesting are those standing against the north wall of the presbytery. They include a headstone inscribed to William Pendrill (or Penderel), who died in 1707 and was the son of the William Penderel who sheltered Charles at Boscobel, and a plain slab with this inscription:

HERE LIETH THE BODIE OF A FRIENDE THE KING DID CALL DAME JOANE BUT NOW SHE IS DECEASED AND GONE INTERRED ANNO DO 1669

This is not the original headstone but a nineteenth-century replica of one found on the site at the end of the eighteenth century. It commemorates Jane Penderel, wife of William Penderel of Boscobel, and, though a copy, it is perhaps the most evocative of all the memorials of those eventful few days of September 1651.

Coronation medal by Thomas Simon, 1661, bearing the words IAM FLORESCIT, "Now it begins to flower"

Further reading

Boscobel House in 1832. By this date stucco had already been applied to the previously half-timbered walls

Charles II's account which he dictated to Samuel Pepys in 1680 was first published by Sir David Dalrymple in 1766 with the title: *An account of the Preservation of King Charles II after the Battle of Worcester, Drawn up by Himself. To which are added His Letters to Several Persons.* It has been republished several times, the most recent edition appearing in 1954 with the title *His Majesty Preserved.*

There are no strictly contemporary accounts of the events of 1651 but a prodigious number of books, pamphlets and broadsheets appeared in 1660 and the years following. Thomas Blount's *Boscobel, or the History of His Sacred Majesty's Most Miraculous Preservation,* first published in 1660 and running into many editions, is a full and detailed account, with a second part added in 1680, but it should be compared with other records which occasionally differ in detail. A number are published in Allan Fea's *After Worcester Fight* (1904) and A M Broadley's *The Royal Miracle* (1912). Thomas Whitgreave's *A Particular Narrative of King Charles II's Concealment at Moseley,* and *A Summary of Occurrences* by Whitgreave and Huddleston are especially useful for events both at Boscobel and at Moseley.

For other works readers are referred to W A Horrox's *Bibliography of Literature relating to the escape and preservation of Charles II after the battle of Worcester,* Aberdeen University Press, 1924.